Johnny Depp

Colleen Adams

Rosen Classroom Books & Materials™
New York

Published in 2006 by The Rosen Publishing Group, Inc.
29 East 21st Street, New York, NY 10010

First Edition

Book Design: Haley Wilson

Photo Credits: Cover © Mike Blake/Reuters/Corbis; pp. 5, 21 © Lisa O'Connor/ ZUMA/Corbis; p. 7 © K Schondorser/Viennareport Agency/Corbis/Sygma; p. 9 © Eric Robert, Stephane Cardinale, & Thierry Orban/Sygma/Corbis; p. 11 © Hulton Archive/Getty Images; p. 13 © Tomo Ikic/ZUMA/Corbis; pp. 15, 17 © Hulton-Deutsch Collection/Corbis; p. 19 © Clive Coote/Miramax Films/Bureau L.A. Collections/Corbis.

Adams, Colleen.
  Johnny Depp / Colleen Adams.
    p. cm. – (The Tony Stead nonfiction independent reading collection)
  Includes index.
  ISBN 1-4042-5667-9
  1. Depp, Johnny–Juvenile literature. 2. Motion picture actors and actresses–United States–Biography–Juvenile literature. I. Title. II. Series.
  PN2287.D39A32 2006
  791.4302'8'092–dc22

                                        2005010023

Manufactured in the United States of America

Contents

Who Is Johnny Depp?

Johnny Depp is a famous actor who has played many different **roles** in movies. You may remember him as the funny pirate, Captain Jack Sparrow, in the movie *Pirates of the Caribbean: The Curse of the Black Pearl*. In the movie *Finding Neverland*, he played J. M. Barrie, the creator and writer of *Peter Pan*. Johnny's characters in these and other movies have earned him Oscar **nominations** as well as other acting honors and **awards**. His ability to create characters that are recognized and easily remembered has made him one of today's best-known actors.

Johnny Depp has created a style of his own.

The Early Years

John Christopher Depp II, the youngest of four children, was born in Owensboro, Kentucky, on June 9, 1963. His family moved to Florida when he was 7. Johnny left high school at the age of 16. He taught himself to play the guitar and spent his time playing in bands that were not well-known. Hoping to become famous, he moved to Los Angeles with a band called The Kids. Johnny struggled to make a living as a **musician**. He made friends with some actors who suggested he try acting.

Johnny still enjoys playing the guitar in his spare time.

7

Early Acting Career

In 1984, Johnny was given a small role in the movie *Nightmare on Elm Street*. His character had a brief but unforgettable part. He was eaten by a bed! Johnny's work as an actor had started. His first big acting break came in 1986. He played the character Officer Tom Hanson on the TV show *21 Jump Street*. The show was written for a teen audience. It was about young police officers working undercover in a school. Johnny played Officer Hanson for 3 years. He became very well known.

Johnny's picture appeared regularly on magazine covers.

9

A Busy Actor

In 1990, Johnny Depp starred in the movie *Edward Scissorhands*. He played a boy who had scissors in place of his hands. Johnny made a name for himself as an actor who wasn't afraid to play strange or unusual characters. He made several more movies in the 1990s. In 1993, he received a Golden Globe nomination as best actor for his role as Sam in *Benny and Joon*. By the end of the 1990s, he had become very successful. Some of the other characters he has played include a movie director, an FBI officer, an **astronaut**, and a writer.

Johnny was nominated for a Golden Globe best actor award for his role in Edward Scissorhands.

11

Captain Jack Sparrow

In the 2003 movie *Pirates of the Caribbean: The Curse of the Black Pearl*, Johnny played Captain Jack Sparrow, a very clever and unusual pirate. He modeled Sparrow's character on a famous musician and a cartoon character. In the movie, Sparrow's ship is stolen by the evil Captain Barbossa. The movie shows the adventures of Sparrow and his friend Will Turner as they try to get his ship back, rescue Turner's childhood friend Elizabeth, and search for lost treasure.

The pirate ship the Black Pearl was specially built for the movie Pirates of the Caribbean.

13

J. M. Barrie

In the 2004 movie *Finding Neverland*, Johnny played the role of Sir James Matthew Barrie, the author of the popular children's story *Peter Pan*. *Peter Pan* is the story of a boy who doesn't want to grow up. Barrie became friends with the five young sons of the Llewelyn-Davies family. He became the person who took care of the boys after their parents died. Peter, one of the Llewelyn-Davies children, is said to have given Barrie the idea to create the main character, Peter Pan. The movie *Finding Neverland* tells the story of Barrie's creative journey writing *Peter Pan*.

This is a picture of author Sir J. M. Barrie, who wrote Peter Pan. Johnny played Barrie in the movie Finding Neverland.

Willy Wonka

In 2005, Johnny starred as Willy Wonka in *Charlie and the Chocolate Factory*. Once again, he added his own personal touch to a character who has been performed by many other actors. *Charlie and the Chocolate Factory* is based on a children's book by Roald Dahl. In the story, Willy Wonka is the owner of a chocolate factory. He meets a boy named Charlie Bucket when Charlie wins a candy contest. Charlie and four other children are taken on a magical tour of the chocolate factory. The story and the movie have many surprises and interesting lessons about life.

This is a picture of author Roald Dahl, who wrote Charlie and the Chocolate Factory.

17

The Role of an Actor

Johnny Depp is able to change his appearance and style to fit the characters he plays. He can appear funny, sad, and even scary. Johnny plays characters who are based on both made-up and real people. He believes that the way he chooses to **represent** a person or character is a very important part of his role as an actor. When playing real people, he believes his character should be played as true as possible to the person. Johnny believes he owes the person and their family his best work.

This picture shows Johnny as J. M. Barrie (third from the left) in a scene from the movie Finding Neverland.

A Family Man

Johnny has two children. Their names are Lily Rose and Jack. Johnny, his children, and their mother, Vanessa Paradis, live in a large country house in southern France. Johnny considers his family the most important part of his life. He believes that Vanessa and his children have helped him to become a better person. When working on a movie, he often travels long distances from the movie set to his home to spend time with his family.

This picture was taken at an awards ceremony. From left to right, it shows Johnny's mother Betty Sue, Johnny, and Vanessa.

What's Next?

After acting in more than forty movies, Johnny Depp continues to take on **challenging** roles. Johnny has said acting is important to him because he enjoys preparing for, creating, and playing different characters. Johnny Depp makes movies because he loves what he does. His fans hope that his interesting characters will be part of movies for a long time to come.

Glossary

astronaut (AS-truh-naht) A person who travels in space.

award (uh-WOHRD) Something that is given to honor an activity.

challenging (CHA-luhn-jing) Interesting and hard.

musician (myoo-ZIH-shun) A person skilled in playing, writing, or singing music.

nomination (nah-muh-NAY-shun) The state of being chosen to be considered for an award or honor.

represent (reh-prih-ZENT) To stand for or be a sign of.

role (ROHL) The character played by an actor.

Index

Web Sites

Due to the changing nature of Internet links, the Rosen
Publishing Group, Inc., has developed an online list of
Web sites related to the subject of this book. This site is
updated regularly. Please use this link to access the list:
http://www.rcbmlinks.com/tsirc/depp/